Microscopic Life
in your
Food

BRIAN WARD

FRANKLIN WATTS
LONDON • SYDNEY

Contents and definitions

Bacteria

Bacteria are far too small to be seen without a microscope. Millions of them live inside you. Bacteria can feed on almost anything, and your own food is ideal for them. Most are harmless, but they can spoil food and sometimes cause serious disease. Bacteria may be rounded, threadlike or rod-shaped, and some of them can move about, using waving threads called flagella.

Mites

Some types of stored foods are attacked by tiny spider-like creatures called mites, usually without causing a great deal of damage. They are harmless to people, except those who have an allergy and are sensitive to the dust they produce.

Fungi

Fungi are small organisms that mostly feed on dead and decaying material. Tiny fungi called yeasts and moulds are used to make many foods we eat. But moulds also cause mildew that damages stored foods, especially in damp conditions.

Viruses

Viruses are even tinier than bacteria, but unlike many bacteria, they must infect a living cell if they are to grow and reproduce. Viruses in your food or drinking water can cause stomach upsets, and plant viruses cause damage to food supplies although they are harmless to people.

Good and bad microbes

The tiny living things we call microbes can be found just about anywhere. It is impossible to keep them out of our food. Sometimes this is a problem — sometimes it is very useful to us.

Wheat is a very important crop. It is vital to keep it clear of bacteria and fungi.

Controlling the bad microbes in food

Cooking is almost the only way to kill completely dangerous microbes in our food. But even if they are destroyed by cooking, they can leave behind poisonous substances that could make you ill. Bacteria and fungi in food are the main threats to health. One solution is to remove them from crops, such as corn and rice, and animals that are used for food, such as chickens and cattle. This is expensive and sometimes means using drugs and chemicals that could themselves be dangerous. It is important that all food is handled and stored very carefully, so these pests can be kept under control.

Handy microbes

Sometimes, we can put these bugs to very good use in changing the flavours in our foods or altering the foods so that they will not spoil. Probably the earliest use of microbes was the discovery thousands of years ago that yeasts growing on fruit or grain such as wheat produce alcohol, and this led to the invention of wine and beer. We still use yeasts for the same purpose, although special types have now been developed to allow them to be used to produce many other substances, for example soy sauce and Marmite.

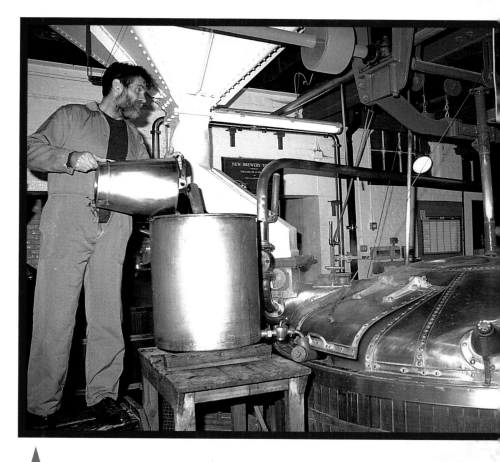

Yeast is added to a fermentation vessel in the beer manufacturing process.

MICRO FACTS

Animal alcohol

Wine and beer have been made with the help of yeast for thousands of years. But even wild animals enjoy alcohol! Yeast grows in some over-ripe fruit to produce alcohol, and animals such as the baboon pictured right sometimes eat so much of this fruit that they become very drunk.

Yeast and fermentation

Yeasts are tiny fungi, far too small to see individually. They are tiny separate cells with thin, fragile walls. Have you ever noticed the whitish layer on the skins of plums and grapes? It is known as 'bloom', and is formed by wild yeast growing on the fruit.

Making alcohol

If fruit is crushed in water, this wild yeast grows very fast, feeding on the sugar in the squashed fruit and producing alcohol. The yeast growth also releases a gas called carbon dioxide (CO_2) — the same gas that forms the bubbles in fizzy drinks. This process is used to make wines and beers, with carefully selected types of yeast to make sure that each batch tastes the same.

Yeast needs sugar in order to grow, but how much? Find out with this simple experiment.

You will need:
- baker's yeast (this can be bought at a supermarket)
- six plastic drinks bottles
- ordinary balloons
- elastic bands

What to do:
1. Put a spoonful of yeast in each bottle, and half-fill the bottles with cold water.
2. Put no sugar in the first bottle, half a teaspoonful in the second bottle, a whole teaspoonful in the next and so on, increasing the amount of sugar each time.
3. Label the bottles so you know how much sugar each one contains, then shake them thoroughly.
4. Stretch the neck of a balloon over the neck of each bottle and wind an elastic band tightly round it to make sure that it will not leak.
5. Put the bottles in a warm place, such as an airing cupboard, and wait for two days. You will see how active the yeast has been by how much the balloons have blown up. Which balloon has blown up the most?

You can also find out if yeast will feed on other common substances. Repeat this experiment using artificial sweetener powder or salt. Do they have any effect on the yeast? Do they create more or less gas than the sugar?

🍞 Bread making

The other main use for yeasts is in making bread, and this, too, has been understood for thousands of years. Live yeast is mixed with flour and water, and the yeast begins to change the flour into sugar on which it feeds and grows. This is called 'fermentation'. It produces a small amount of alcohol, but larger quantities of the gas carbon dioxide. This gas is trapped in the sticky dough, making bubbles that cause it to swell up or 'rise'. Once the dough has risen, it is baked in an oven, and the high temperature kills the yeast and removes the alcohol and carbon dioxide, leaving lots of small holes that make the bread soft and light. Bread made without yeast is flat and often hard.

Yeast feeds on the sugar in bread dough, producing tiny gas bubbles that make the dough swell up or 'rise'.

Many different types of bread can be made by using different types of flour and additives.

7

Fermented foods

Fermentation is not just used to make alcoholic drinks and bread. It is a process used to preserve many foods to prevent them spoiling, to add flavour and to produce new food substances.

Vinegar can be produced by continuing the fermentation process. ▶

⬢ Making vinegar

Yeasts produce alcohol by fermenting sugars, but are eventually killed by the alcohol they produce. The process can be continued by adding other bacteria called *Acetobacter* to the mixture. These convert the alcohol to an acid called acetic acid, which you know better as the main substance in vinegar. Wine sometimes becomes vinegary, because the cork has not been pushed properly into the bottle and bacteria get in.

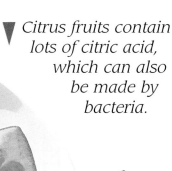

▼ *Citrus fruits contain lots of citric acid, which can also be made by bacteria.*

⬢ Citric acid

You will recognise the sharp taste of citric acid, which is found in most fruit, especially citrus fruits such as oranges and lemons. It is often added to fizzy drinks. Citric acid is made in huge quantities in factories, fermenting sugars and other substances with moulds called *Aspergillus*.

🔹 Pickled and preserved foods

The popular German food sauerkraut is made by fermenting cabbage. The cabbage is preserved by the acid that is produced, so it can be kept for much longer than fresh cabbage. Sometimes 'bad' bacteria can make meat dangerous to eat, but if the right bacteria are present, they can preserve meat for a long time. Sausages such as salami are preserved in this way. The 'good' bacteria produce substances that prevent the growth of other bacteria that would cause the meat to decay and go off.

Fermentation by bacteria helps preserve salami sausage, as well as giving it a characteristic taste.

MICRO FACTS

Tasty soya

The typical taste of Chinese and other oriental foods is the result of fermentation, used to make spicy soy sauce. It is made by fermenting crushed soya beans and wheat with a mould, producing a brown salty liquid that is used to season the food. Soya beans are also fermented to make a smelly and sticky food, popular in Japan, called natto. A form of tofu (fermented soya bean curd) is used as a meat substitute in many vegetarian foods.

🔹 Industry and fermentation

Fermentation is sometimes used to speed up food processes in industry. Coffee beans and cocoa used to make chocolate are both fermented to soften the pulpy fruit and make it easier to process the inside of the beans.

Fungal foods

When you think of a fungus, do you think of mushrooms? Most fungi are much smaller, sometimes even too small to see without a microscope.

Tiny tangled threads called hyphae spread through the material on which fungi feed.

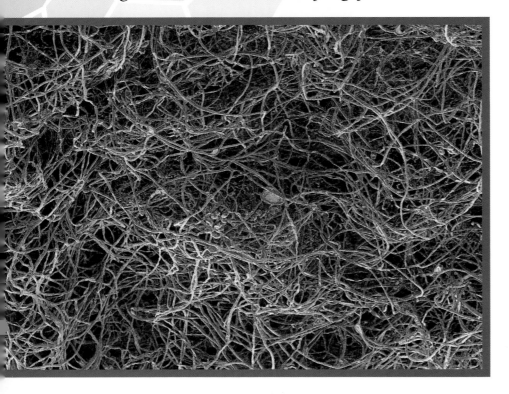

Hiding underground

Certain types of fungi push up mushrooms when they reproduce. The main parts of the fungi are found beneath the ground. These are tiny threads called hyphae, which spread through the soil or the material they are feeding on.

Because of their taste, some mushrooms are popular foods, although they contain very little nourishment that our bodies can use. Several different types of mushrooms are sold in food stores, each having its own taste.

MICRO FACTS

A giant under the ground
The biggest living thing in the world is a fungus called *Armillaria*. This particular fungus lives in the USA, and it is 5.6 km across, though most of it is hidden underground. The giant fungus is probably hundreds of years old.

Designer fungi

Recently scientists developed an entirely new type of food, based on fungi. This new food was designed in a laboratory to be used instead of expensive meat so it could be given to people threatened by famine in poor countries. The scientists wanted to produce a food that would be just as good for people as meat but much cheaper to produce. This new food also had to taste and feel like meat when it was chewed.

These are the fine threads of Fusarium fungus, the natural fungus that became the basis of a new type of food.

The main ingredient of these wraps is 'Quorn'®. From its appearance, it could easily be mistaken for meat.

A natural fungus called *Fusarium* was discovered, which was grown in huge amounts in a complicated industrial process. The new food material, now named 'Quorn'®, looks and tastes so much like meat that some vegetarians refuse to eat it. It is often used in prepared foods such as 'meat' pies. Look out for Quorn in your local supermarket.

Helpful bacteria

Like yeast, bacteria can be very useful in making our foods. The process often starts accidentally in our own homes.

▲ *Bacterial fermentation has caused the milk in this bottle to separate into solid and liquid parts.*

◆ Why does milk go sour?

After a few days, milk begins to go sour even when it is kept in the refrigerator. Souring is caused by bacteria called *Lactobacillus* and other bacteria that are already in the milk. The bacteria feed on a form of milk sugar called lactose, and turn it into lactic acid. This has the sharp, sour taste of milk that is 'going off'. Usually we throw this milk away, but it is only the first part of a process that leads to many common tasty foods, such as sour cream, cottage cheese, crème fraîche and yoghurt.

MICRO FACTS

Nursery rhyme knowledge

'Little Miss Muffet sat on her tuffet, Eating her curds and whey...'

When milk sours, it separates into curds and whey. Curds are the solid material that sinks. Whey is the clear liquid above it. Both curds and whey contain valuable food substances, although you might not like their taste!

Cheese making

Cheese is made by adding special cultures of bacteria to milk to sour it. As the bacteria makes more and more lactic acid, the milk thickens and the curds settle at the bottom of the container. The whey above is strained off, and the curds are squeezed dry and stored, sometimes for several years. During storage, the bacteria gradually change the taste of the curds and produce 'ripe' cheese. Tiny fungi called moulds may be added to some cheeses such as Stilton to change their taste even more, producing bluish streaks in the cheese. Some moulds produce large holes like those you see in Gruyère cheese, when gas bubbles form.

▲ *Cheese produced by bacterial action on milk is stored to mature and improve its flavour.*

Killing the bugs

The milk you use at home is usually heat-treated in a process called pasteurisation to kill most of the bacteria it contains. This makes it safe to drink and delays souring. Some people prefer the taste of untreated milk, but it can be dangerous to drink as it might carry disease-producing bacteria spread from infected cows.

▼ *Different types of bacteria produce cheeses with very different tastes.*

13

Mould and mildew

Mildew is a coloured layer of tiny fluffy fungi called moulds. You may have seen mildew growing on damp walls, especially in bathrooms, forming a black or greenish layer.

Mouldy food

Mould can also contaminate food and make it dangerous to eat. You might see moulds growing on damp bread that has been kept for a while, or forming a greenish skin on the surface of a pot of jam that has not had the lid firmly screwed down.

Fluffy patches of mould are produced by tiny fungi growing on food such as bread.

TRY IT YOURSELF

Make mouldy bread!

Mould spores carried in the air quickly infect damp bread, but some types grow faster than others. You can see this for yourself. Put a piece of damp bread in a snap-top plastic bag and keep it in a warm place. Check it every day and write down what you see — but never open the bag, even though it may become difficult to see through. Different coloured moulds will appear and die off, until the whole piece of bread is reduced to a sticky mess. When you are finished with it, throw the bag away without opening it, so you don't breathe in any of the microscopic mould spores. These can make some people ill.

What are moulds?

Moulds are made of tiny fungus 'threads' that spread through food. The threads are so fine they look invisible. Moulds feed by releasing chemicals into the food around them, softening it so it can be absorbed. You only notice them when they reproduce, producing tiny stalks, each tipped with a structure containing microscopic spores. These spores will be carried in the air and if they fall in certain places they will grow, spreading the mould. The spores are usually black or green, but they can be any colour. Mildew makes food taste musty. It means that the food is decaying, and there is probably bacteria too, so mildewy food must always be thrown away. *Aspergillus* is a common mould in food that sometimes damages huge stores of crops.

Mucor is a mould that produces grey patches on bread and other food.

Moulds for health

Penicillium is one of the commonest moulds growing on food, and it was one of these moulds that was accidentally found to contain the first known antibiotic, penicillin. The discovery of this natural substance has since saved the lives of millions of people infected with dangerous bacteria.

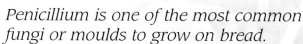

Penicillium is one of the most common fungi or moulds to grow on bread.

15

Costly microbes

Every year, a quarter of all of our stored food is spoiled by fungus infection or eaten by insect pests, and this is very expensive.

Threat to food

The threat of microbe damage means that crops are often sprayed with expensive chemicals, and that food storage becomes more expensive. Some food such as wheat can be heated to dry it out and prevent the growth of moulds and other fungi, but vegetables such as potatoes are more difficult to protect. Traditionally, potatoes are stacked up after harvesting, and covered over to protect them from bad weather. But this means that any moisture on the potatoes cannot escape, forming a warm, damp environment in which fungi love to grow. If the potatoes have been damaged during harvesting, the fungal threads can get in very easily.

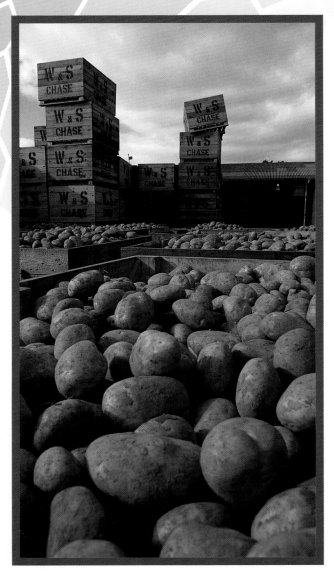

▲ *The thin skins of potatoes are easily damaged during harvesting, allowing fungi to get in and cause decay.*

MICRO FACTS Famine tragedy

A fungal disease of potatoes, called potato blight, caused a tragedy in the 19th century. More than a million people in Ireland died from starvation when the potato crop failed over several years. Potatoes were so easy to grow that they had become the main diet for poor people in Ireland, and when the blight destroyed all of the crops in the fields, the people starved because they had no other food. The Great Potato Famine caused nearly two million Irish people to abandon their farms and emigrate, mostly to the USA.

Dangerous moulds

Moulds that attack stored food can cause serious illness. For instance, it was found that mould growing on peanuts that were stored badly produced chemicals that could cause cancer of the liver. *Aspergillus* is a common mould that sometimes causes this disease.

Aspergillus produces millions of tiny airborne spores from its packed fruiting bodies.

Canned bugs

Some types of bacteria grow well in conditions where there is no oxygen from the air, such as in tins or sealed jars. Tinned or bottled food has to be heat-treated properly to kill any microbes in the food. Botulism is a serious disease, caused by a bacterium called *Clostridium*. It occurs sometimes when people preserve food they have made in glass jars that have not been sealed properly. Very dangerous bacterial infections such as typhoid have been spread by canned foods that were not properly sealed. It is not safe to use food from damaged cans.

Food cans must be airtight to keep out dangerous bacteria.

Bad bugs

Billions of microbes live in your intestines, helping you to digest your food. But sometimes these bugs can turn nasty, or a bad bug may get into your system, making you ill.

E. coli. Friend or enemy?

Escherichia coli (usually known as *E. coli*) are common bacteria causing lots of stomach complaints. These normally live in your intestines, where they do not harm you because your body has become used to them. But when you go on holiday, you may encounter a different strain of *E. coli* that could make you ill for a while. *E. coli* is usually spread by poor hygiene, when an infected person does not wash their hands thoroughly after using the toilet, and then goes on to handle food. It may also spread when sewage gets into water where people swim.

Tiny hairs on E. coli bacteria help them to move about and to stick to the gut wall.

New types of bug

Humans are pretty tough, and bacteria picked up in our food usually do not cause anything more serious than a short dose of diarrhoea. But recently, a new strain of *E. coli* appeared that caused outbreaks of illness where large numbers of people became infected, and some were very ill indeed. One recent outbreak affected a group of elderly people who ate meat pies supplied by a local butcher, and several of them died. The outbreak was found to have been caused by poor hygiene at the shop where the pies were made.

Bugs in your burger?

Salmonella is the most common bug causing food poisoning, but recently another dangerous type of bacteria has created health problems. This bug, called *Campylobacter*, is spread by undercooked meat, and it can cause very severe diarrhoea lasting for a long time. Part-cooked meat can also sometimes contain other dangerous organisms such as tape worms!

It is important to cook ▶ *meat thoroughly to kill the bacteria it contains.*

MICRO FACTS

Who needs to avoid *Listeria*?

Listeria are common bacteria, found in nearly 1 person in every 10 people. They are also present in milk that has not been heat-treated, cheese made from such milk, and in many types of vegetables and raw meat. Usually we can eat these foods without any problems. But pregnant women and some people with serious medical conditions have to avoid these foods, because their bodies' natural defences are unable to fight off large numbers of these bacteria, which could then cause dangerous illness. In pregnancy, this is particularly threatening to the unborn child.

Attack of the mites

You might have seen large salami sausages hanging up in a delicatessen or supermarket, covered with a dusty grey layer. Or very ripe cheese with a thick grey crust on the outside. You might have enjoyed eating these foods.

Feeding on bugs

Now here's something you won't like. That dusty grey layer on salami and ripe cheese is a mixture of all sorts of bugs, and it probably contains masses of tiny eight-legged creepy crawlies called mites, together with their dust-like droppings. Mites are tiny relatives of spiders. They are so small as to be almost invisible, and they do not seem to do any harm at all, although some people are allergic to their dust. Some cheeses are given a thin coating of hard wax to stop the mites from living on them. There are even some cheeses that depend on huge numbers of these mites to give them their flavour!

Mites are often responsible for the powdery appearance of the rind of mature cheeses or of salami.

Mites in your food cupboard

Because mites are so tiny, they spread easily. There are different types of mites that feed on almost any food stored in your home, including flour, dried milk, cereals and preserved fruit. Although they do not do much harm, mites are unpleasant. Their presence usually means that food is not being stored properly, and is likely to be damp.

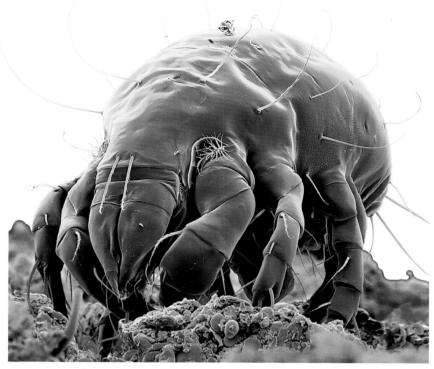

Tiny spider-like mites feed on almost any stored foods.

Look for mites

If you can borrow a powerful magnifying glass, or better still use a microscope, you may be able to see mites in food. Look for dust at the back of food cupboards, or try scraping some of the powdery crust from strong cheese, or parts of the blue veins in 'blue' cheese, and take a close look. The mites are usually a pale brown or cream colour, and you might be able to see them moving about. Wash your hands carefully afterwards, because some people are allergic to mites.

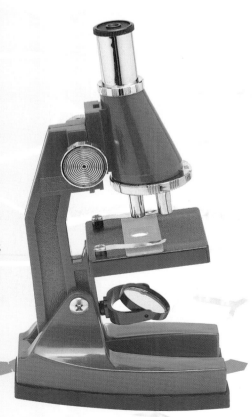

Healthy food?

Animals used for food may develop many serious diseases, but they do not usually cause health problems for humans. However, they can still be very expensive for farmers.

Foot and mouth disease is the most infectious viral disease known, and it sometimes causes epidemics among farm animals. ▶

Foot and mouth

Foot and mouth disease is caused by a virus. It affects all types of animals with hooves (apart from horses). It makes them sick but does not usually kill them. However, farmers are unable to sell the infected animals. Because it is the most infectious disease known, at present the best way to get rid of it is to kill every infected animal before they can spread the disease. This is enormously expensive so vaccine alternatives are being developed.

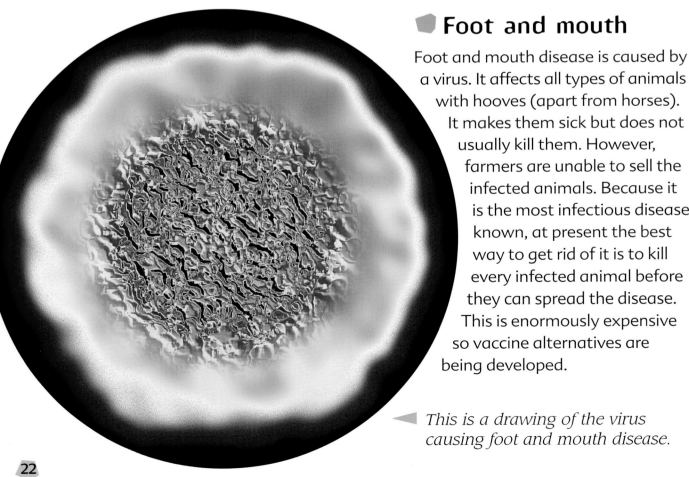

◀ *This is a drawing of the virus causing foot and mouth disease.*

Why does milk need heat treatment?

Diseases such as tuberculosis (TB) were once spread through drinking the milk from infected cows. Now we usually drink pasteurised milk that has been heated for a short time to make it safe.

BSE and New Variant CJD both cause brain tissue to become spongy, as shown by the white spaces in this section of an infected brain.

Brain disease

BSE or mad cow disease probably started as a disease of sheep, called scrapie. This has been around for centuries, but recently farmers started to add parts of slaughtered infected sheep to cattle feed, and the infection seems to have 'jumped' to cattle, which up until then had not been infected. A very similar disease called Kuru once affected cannibals in Papua New Guinea, who sometimes ate the brains of infected people and then became ill themselves.

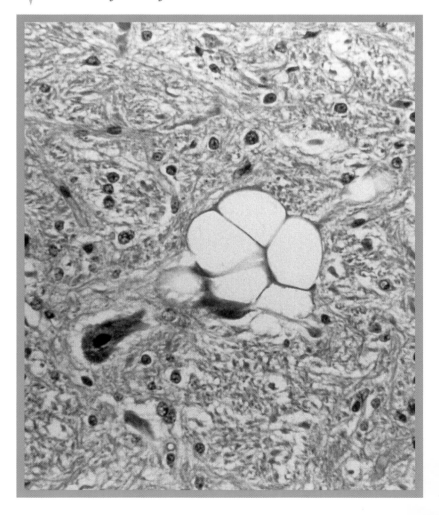

The threat from beef

One very dangerous disease has recently appeared, infecting cattle and occasionally spreading to people eating beef. It is called Bovine Spongiform Encephalopathy, or BSE, and the human form is called New Variant CJD. BSE is a mysterious brain disease that seems to be spread by something called a prion. This is not a living bug at all, although it behaves very much like a normal infection. Like many other livestock diseases, BSE is controlled by slaughtering all of the infected animals, though it may take a long time before all risk is gone.

Safe food storage

One of the commonest threats to health in the home is food that has not been stored properly, or has not been handled in a hygienic way.

The need for a refrigerator

All uncooked foods are covered with bacteria, most of which are harmless. But in warm conditions, the bacteria will grow faster, so food needs to be kept refrigerated to slow down the bacteria's growth. Even keeping food in the refrigerator does not mean it will keep for long, as some bacteria can live and grow even at low temperatures. All food is best kept in closed containers, where bugs in the air cannot reach them.

Raw meat must be kept well away from cooked meat to avoid bacterial contamination.

Cooked and raw foods must be kept apart in the refrigerator.

Danger from chickens

Bacteria growing on meat are a serious health problem. Many chickens and their eggs are contaminated with bacteria called *Salmonella*. These do not cause the living chickens much of a problem, but the bacteria continue to grow in chickens' meat and eggs. This can produce a poison called a toxin. The bacteria are destroyed if the meat or eggs are cooked thoroughly, but the toxin may remain there even after cooking, and can cause violent diarrhoea when the food is eaten.

Keep away from raw meat!

It is very important that raw meat is kept well away from cooked meat and other foods, as the live bacteria could quickly spread to them. Chefs in restaurants have to keep raw and cooked meats in different refrigerators, and even have to use separate knives for preparing the foods. At home, you should take care to wash chopping boards, knives and hands thoroughly when preparing food.

Kitchen hygiene is very important to prevent the spread of disease.

Freshly cooked food is best

Freezing can preserve foods for a very long time, because at very low temperatures the bacteria cannot reproduce. However, as soon as the food is thawed the bacteria become active again and start to produce toxins, so it is dangerous to refreeze food once it has been thawed out. The same thing can happen if food is heated again after it has been cooked and allowed to cool down. Bacteria grow very fast in the warm food. Freshly cooked food tastes better anyway, and is far safer!

MICRO FACTS
How many ways are there to preserve food safely?

Refrigeration and freezing: slows or prevents the growth of microbes.
Canning: food is cooked in the sealed can to kill microbes.
Radiation: can be used to kill microbes in sealed packets.
Freeze-drying: water is removed from frozen food.
Salting and pickling: salt slows or prevents the growth of microbes; so does acetic acid (vinegar).
Fermentation: using yeast or bacteria.
Chemical preservatives: factory-made substances that slow or prevent the growth of microbes.

Fly alert

Flies can be irritating when they buzz around you, but sometimes they can be dangerous, too.

House flies feed and lay their eggs on decaying matter that is full of bacteria. ▼

🔹 Flies are filthy!

Just think for a minute about how flies live. They love to buzz around dead or decaying material. They are attracted by the smell and feed on it, and lay their eggs there. Flies feed by vomiting up substances called enzymes on to their food. Enzymes attack and soften the food, turning it to liquid. The fly then sucks up this partly digested liquid. Then it buzzes away and the next time it lands could be on your food, or on the edge of the glass you are about to drink from. If you see a fly landing somewhere near you, watch it and notice what it does.

Bugs on their feet

The fly's feet and legs are covered in bristly hairs. As it cleans itself, the fly rubs its legs all over its body, so the whole surface of the fly becomes covered with millions of bacteria that were picked up when it walked in its last meal. It is going to spread these bacteria all over your food if it gets the chance to walk about on it. Ordinary houseflies carry at least 100 different types of disease-producing microbes, some of which are very dangerous.

What could you catch from a fly?

You probably won't catch anything nasty from flies if you live in a cool climate. But in the tropics, these are some of the diseases spread by flies:

- **dysentery**
- **food poisoning**
- **cholera**
- **worm parasites**
- **polio**
- **eye infection.**

Always be careful to keep flies away from food when eating outdoors.

Holiday hazards

Although they are unpleasant, flies do not usually cause us too many health problems. But if you visit a hot country, or places where hygiene is poor, flies can be a real risk to health. However careful you are about storing or preparing your food, one fly can give you a big dose of bugs such as *Salmonella*, and there may be enough bacteria present to make you so ill that it can spoil your holiday. Never leave your food uncovered, and make sure you shoo any flies away if they look like landing in your dinner.

Keeping clean

The simplest way to avoid becoming infected by food bugs is to make sure that you do not meet them, or at least do not meet too many of them. The best approach is to be hygienic when you eat or prepare food, but there are also other precautions you can take.

◆ Bug killing

Heat is the most effective way to sterilise food (this means, to kill the bacteria it contains). High temperatures kill bugs. Moist heat like steam is better at killing bacteria than dry heat, and nearly all bacteria are killed by boiling or roasting for a while. This is part of the normal cooking process. The flavour of milk is changed if it is boiled, so the process of pasteurisation is carried out at a lower temperature and for only a short time. This is why a few bugs always remain and will eventually sour the milk.

◀

Kitchens must be kept spotless to avoid infection.

The bug threat to babies

It is particularly important to clean babies' feeding bottles very thoroughly, because dried-up milk is a very good place for bacteria to grow. Even small amounts of bacteria can cause sickness in a baby, who will not yet have become used to all of the common bugs. Bottles are usually soaked in special chemicals to make sure they are thoroughly clean.

It is almost impossible to remove all of the bugs from food, or from the food preparation areas of a kitchen. But most of them can be killed by cleaning up with household bleach. This strong-smelling liquid releases poisonous chlorine, which can kill almost any form of microbe life.

Work surfaces and sinks are often heavily contaminated with bacteria.

Why you need to scrub your hands

You probably wash your hands thoroughly to get rid of germs after you use the toilet. But have you really got rid of them? To see just how hard it is to get your hands really clean, brush water-based ink or paint over your hand and let it dry. Now try to wash it off with cold water, then warm water, and finally, with warm water and soap.

Did you manage to remove every trace? Even from under your fingernails? Then just think: bacteria are so small, they can get into the roughened surface of your skin, just like the ink or paint, and will be just as hard to dislodge. Even harder, because you will not be able to see whether you have got rid of them.

Glossary

Acetobacter: Type of bacteria that converts alcohol into acetic acid, in the process used to make vinegar.

Alcohol: Substance produced by yeast when it feeds on sugar.

Allergy: Body reaction to a harmless substance such as a type of food or pollen in the air.

Antibiotic: Drug that kills or attacks bacteria.

Aspergillus: Type of fungus that commonly causes food to spoil.

Bacteria: Tiny single-celled microbes that live nearly everywhere, including people's bodies, food and homes. Some bacteria can be 'good', for example helping people to digest food. Other bacteria can be 'bad', because they cause diseases.

BSE: Bovine Spongiform Encephalopathy; usually known as Mad Cow Disease. An infection of cattle that can sometimes spread to humans, causing brain damage.

Campylobacter: Type of bacteria that can cause a very severe infection of the digestive system. It is carried in contaminated meat.

Carbon dioxide (CO_2): Colourless gas that is a waste product of the body. It is also produced by the fermentation of sugar by yeast.

Chlorine: Pungent gas that is released by bleach. It is used to disinfect sinks and work surfaces. Chlorine kills most micro-organisms.

CJD: Creutzfeld Jacob Disease; the human form of Mad Cow Disease.

Curds: Solid material left when milk is soured by the action of bacteria.

Dysentery: Very severe diarrhoea, caused by infection with bacteria.

Environment: The surroundings of a living organism.

Enzymes: Substances produced by a living creature that help to digest food.

Escherichia coli (E. coli): Common bacteria living in the gut that sometimes cause disease.

Fermentation: Process in which a microbe breaks down food substances, often producing useful materials at the same time.

Flagella: Thin hair-like strands found on some bacteria and other microbes. They allow the microbe to move about.

Freeze drying: Removal of water at very low temperatures. This process is often used to preserve food.

Fungus: Organism that breaks down dead material and sometimes also causes diseases. Most fungi are microscopic; others are large, such as mushrooms.

Lactic acid: Sour-tasting substance produced when bacteria cause milk to 'go off'.

Lactobacillus: The most common of the bacteria that cause milk to become sour.

Livestock: Farm animals.

Mad Cow Disease: See BSE.

Mildew: Layer of tiny fungi (moulds) growing on a damp surface.

Mites: Tiny spider-like animals that feed on skin flakes, food debris or sometimes people.

Moulds: Fungi that often attack stored foods, especially when they are damp. Very common on stale bread.

Natto: Oriental food produced by fermenting soya.

Oxygen: Colourless gas in the air we breathe.

Pasteurisation: Process in which milk is quickly heated to destroy dangerous bacteria and to delay souring.

Penicillin: Antibiotic produced by a mould.

Penicillium: The type of mould that produces penicillin. It commonly grows on stale bread.

Pickling: Preserving food by fermenting it so that the substances produced prevent further microbe growth.

Polio: A serious virus infection that can cause paralysis. The virus is spread by contaminated water. Now very rare, because of vaccination.

Prion: A chemical substance that has some of the properties of living things. A prion is thought to be responsible for the brain disease BSE.

Quorn®: A food substance produced from fungi, and widely used as a substitute for meat.

Salmonella: Bacteria that are commonly responsible for food poisoning. The bacteria live in chickens, eggs and other farm livestock, and can be killed by thorough cooking.

Sauerkraut: German food, made of fermented cabbage.

Soya beans: Important food source, used to make flour, and fermented to make several other types of foods.

Spores: Tiny cells which drift through the air. Spores spread fungi and bacteria.

Toxin: Poisonous substance produced by some bacteria.

Tuberculosis (TB): A serious disease caused by bacteria, which mostly attacks the lungs. It can be prevented by vaccination.

Vaccination: Process that produces immunity to an infection.

Virus: Very simple organism that can only grow and reproduce inside a living cell. All viruses are parasites.

Whey: Clear liquid left above the curds after milk has soured.

Yeast: Tiny fungi, usually with a single cell. Yeasts are important in making alcoholic drinks and causing bread to rise.

Further information

The following web sites contain lots of useful information about microbes and their effects on the body:

Microbiology on-line:
www.microbiologyonline.org.uk/wom.htm

Microbe Zoo:
www.commtechlab.msu.edu/sites/dlc-me/zoo

Microbe World:
www.microbeworld.org

Microbes — invisible invaders, amazing allies:
www.miamisci.org/microbes/facts18.html

Stalking the mysterious microbe:
www.microbe.org

Good bacteria in food:
www.bacteriamuseum.org/niches/food safety/goodfood.shtml

index

First published in 2003
by Franklin Watts
96 Leonard Street
LONDON EC2A 4XD

Franklin Watts Australia
45–51 Huntley Street
Alexandria
NSW 2015

© 2003 Franklin Watts

A CIP catalogue record for this book is available from the British Library

ISBN: 0 7496 4792 2

Printed in Hong Kong, China

Editor: Kate Banham
Designer: Joelle Wheelwright
Art direction: Peter Scoulding
Picture research: Diana Morris
Educational consultant: Dot Jackson

Acknowledgements

The publishers would like to thank the following for permission to reproduce photographs in this book:
Sean Aidan/Eye Ubiquitous: 22t. Anthony Bannister/Corbis: front cover bl, b cover tl. Martin Brigdale/ABPL: 28. Howard Brundrett/Eye Ubiquitous: 4, 16. Dr. Jeremy Burgess/SPL: 3t,11b. Martyn F. Chillmaid/SPL: 12l. CNEVA/SPL: 23b. Eye of Science/SPL: fr cover cr.2t, 17tr, 18. Tim Hawkins/Eye Ubiquitous: 13t. Tim Hill/ABPL: 8t. Jim Hulme/Eye Ubiquitous: 5t. Tim Macpherson/ABPL: 25. Maximillian/ABPL: 13b. Microfield Scientific Ltd/SPL: 15b. Cordelia Molloy/SPL: 14. Claude Nuridsany & Marie Perennou/SPL: 15t. Alfred Pasieka/SPL: 3b, 22b. J.B. Pickering/Eye Ubiquitous: 6. Fritz Polking/FLPA: 5. © Quorn/Marlow Foods Ltd.:11t. RDL/ABPL: 20. Rosenfeld Images/ABPL: 9t. David Scharf/SPL: 10. Science Pictures Ltd/SPL: 2b, 21t. Paul Seheult/Eye Ubiquitous: 19. Ariel Skelley/Corbis: 27b.

Whilst every attempt has been made to clear copyright should there be any inadvertent omission please apply in the first instance to the publisher regarding rectification.